Introductio

What better way of whiling away the cold
a glass of hot punch and the comforting cr
While endless cups of hot tea, coffee and
substitutes during the weekdays, why not t
the punches featured in this book when it
Your will be spoiled for choice. There are
tional favourites like whisky, rum and bro
unusual concoctions including Calvados, apple brandy or Poires
William, a pear liqueur.

Written by Tim Cole

This edition published 1994 by Merehurst Limited
Ferry House, 51-57 Lacy Road,
Putney, London SW15 1PR

Copyright © Gräfe und Unzer GmbH 1991, Munich

ISBN 1 874567 71 9

All rights reserved

Designed by Clive Dorman & Co.
Printed in Italy by G. Canale & C.S.p.A

Distributed in the UK by J.B. Fairfax Press Limited,
9 Trinity Centre, Park Farm, Wellingborough, Northants NN8 6ZB

Distributed in Australia by J.B. Fairfax Press Pty Ltd,
80 McLachlan Avenue, Rushcutters Bay, Sydney, NSW 2011

Glögg

Pronounced Glurg, this is Scandinavia's answer to winter's extremes.

20 cardamom pods
1 orange
2 litres (3½ pints/8 cups) strong red wine
1 cinnamon stick
25 cloves
155g (5oz) raisins or sultanas
155g (5oz) blanched almonds
560ml (18fl oz/2 ¼ cups) brandy or aquavit
15 sugar cubes

EXTRAS
1 small and 1 large saucepan
1 bain marie
1 wire mesh 'lid' for saucepan (usually
   handled)
Heatproof glasses or mugs

1 Break each cardamom pod by
tapping it with a knife handle. Open
out to reveal tiny black seeds. Peel orange
and cut into thin strips. Put cardamon seeds
and peel into a large saucepan.

2 Pour in wine then add cinnamon and
cloves. Bring slowly to the boil. Cover
and keep hot over a low heat.

3 After 15 minutes, add raisins or sultanas
and almonds. Cover and continue to
heat slowly for a further 15 minutes.

4 Pour the brandy or aquavit into a small
saucepan and heat gently, until warm
taking care not to boil.

5 Transfer the large saucepan of Glögg
to a bain marie containing about 10cm
(4ins) of gently simmering water. This will
keep the drink hot.

6 Cover saucepan with mesh lid and
arrange sugar cubes on top. Spoon
warm brandy or aquavit over the sugar then
carefully set alight with a match. The flaming sugar will gradually melt and fall through
the mesh into the saucepan.

7 Ladle punch into glasses or mugs as
soon as all the sugar has dissolved. Each
glass should contain 2 raisins or sultanas and
2 almonds.

THE PHARISEE
A favourite drink with the people of
Germany's North Sea Coast (Friesland) is a
legendary drink called The Pharisee. It is
composed of a tot of rum washed down
with strong, sweetened coffee topped with
thick whipped cream.

Glögg

Hot Buttered Rum

Makes 1 drink

An après-ski drink from the USA.

1 cube of sugar
3 tablespoons dark rum
1 teaspoon butter
Freshly grated nutmeg

EXTRAS
1 heavy whisky glass or 1 mug

1 Warm the glass or mug.

2 Put in the sugar then two-thirds fill the glass with hot water.

3 Add rum and butter and stir until butter melts.

4 Sprinkle with nutmeg and drink straight away.

HOT TODDY
Toddy is another name for fermented palm tree sap and also the basis of a group of Asiatic drinks brought to Holland and England by old Colonials.

To make a simple Toddy, put some sugar, hot water and a generous measure of your favourite alcohol into a warm glass. Add a slice of lemon, 2-3 cloves, stir round and serve.

Hot Buttered Rum

Grog

Makes 1 drink

The perfect drink to warm you up on a cold winter's evening.

1 cube of sugar
3½ tablespoons dark rum
2 tablespoons whipped cream (optional)

EXTRAS
1 heatproof glass or mug
1 long-handled spoon

1 Drop sugar cube into the glass or mug then three-quarters fill with boiling water.

2 Add rum then stir until sugar has completely dissolved.

3 Stir in cream, if using, and serve straight away.

THROWING A GROG PARTY...
Have heatproof glasses or mugs ready on mats with a saucepan of pre-warmed rum, a bowl of sugar cubes and a second pan of boiling water. Allow your guests to prepare their own drinks – proportions of alcohol to water is then a matter of personal taste and is a good way for drivers to monitor their alcohol intake.

Grog

Mulled Wine

Makes 1 drink

An old-fashioned, soothing drink often served at Christmas time.

10 sultanas
3½ tablespoons dark rum
250ml (8fl oz/1 cup) white wine
1 teaspoon caster sugar
Pinch of ground cinnamon
Slice of orange

EXTRAS
1 small bowl
1 small saucepan
1 heatproof glass or mug

1 Tip sultanas into bowl, add rum, cover and leave to soak for 1 hour.

2 Transfer punch to saucepan. Pour in wine then add sugar and cinnamon.

3 Heat punch, without boiling, stirring until sugar dissolves. Pour into glass and decorate rim with orange slice.

FRUITY MULLED WINE
Add a few blanched almonds and some chopped dried fruits, such as figs, apricots, dates and pears to each glass. Serve with spoons so that the fruit can be eaten separately.

Mulled Wine

Uncle Charlie

Makes 1 drink

A cross between Grog and Mulled Wine, this punch is sure to become a favourite.

10 sultanas
3½ tablespoons dark rum
250ml (8 fl oz/1 cup) white wine
1 teaspoon caster sugar
Pinch of ground cinnamon
Slice of orange

EXTRAS
1 small bowl
1 small saucepan
1 heatproof glass or mug

1 Tip sultanas into bowl, add rum, cover and leave to soak for 1 hour.

2 Transfer punch to saucepan. Pour in wine then add sugar and cinnamon.

3 Heat punch, without boiling, stirring until sugar dissolves. Pour into glass and decorate rim with orange slice.

UNCLE CHARLIE WITHOUT ALCOHOL
Make 315ml (10fl oz/1¼ cups) tea with tea bags and boiling water and leave to brew for 5 minutes. Put 3 tablespoons cherry or blackcurrant fruit juice into a saucepan with 1 tablespoon of lemon juice, 1 clove and 1 cinnamon stick. Add tea then re-heat without boiling. Strain into a heatproof glass or mug and drink piping hot.

Uncle Charlie

Hunter's Tea

Makes 1 drink

A version of the Tyrol's national cold weather drink.

315ml (10fl oz/1¼ cups) freshly-made strong
   tea
4 tablespoons dry white wine
2 tablespoons dark rum
2 tablespoons colourless fruit liqueur such as
   kirsch or Poires William
Sugar cubes

EXTRAS
1 small teapot
1 heatproof glass

1 Make tea in teapot and leave to stand
for 5 minutes.

2 Pour wine into glass then add rum, fruit
liqueur and sugar to taste.

3 Strain tea into the wine mixture then stir
until sugar dissolves.

DANISH COFFEE PUNCH
This punch is a traditional Danish drink. Make
a jug of strong coffee, basing the amount
on the number of people to be served. Add
a newly-minted 10-Ore coin (use well-
washed pennies instead) to each heatproof
glass. Add coffee until the coins seem to
disappear. Next pour in sufficient Aquavit
(Denmark's national drink) until the coins re-
appear. Drink while still hot.

Hunter's Tea

Hot Sangria

Serves 8-10

Bring summer to winter with a favourite from Spain. This version contains pieces of dried fruit and almonds.

155ml (5fl oz/⅔ cup) brandy
625ml (1 pint/2½ cups) apple juice
2 bottles of dry red wine
375g (12oz) mixed dried fruit including apricots, peaches and pears, well-washed
2 tablespoons blanched almonds
2 medium oranges, sliced

EXTRAS
1 large saucepan
1 pair kitchen scissors
1 ladle
Heatproof tumblers

1 Pour brandy into saucepan with apple juice and wine.

2 Cut fruit into small pieces with scissors (dip them in and out of hot water to prevent the fruit from sticking). Add to pan with almonds and orange slices.

3 Heat punch until hot, but do not allow to boil. Ladle into glasses, adding pieces of fruit and nuts to each. Serve with a spoon in each for eating the fruit and nuts separately.

DON'T BOIL...
Spirits contain not only alcohol but also natural flavouring oils which are sometimes aromatic too. Boiling has an adverse effect on flavour so hot punches should be heated until hot, never boiled.

Hot Sangria

Step-by-step

WARMING PUNCH GLASSES

1 For a warm glass, rinse under hot running tap water for 30 seconds.

2 For a hot glass be sure to use a heatproof glass. Fill with boiling water and leave to stand for 1 minute. Empty and wipe dry.

3 For slow warming of glasses, put into a saucepan containing 5cm (2ins) of lukewarm water. Leave over a moderate heat until water starts to steam. Switch off heat, lift out glasses and wipe dry.

1

BLANCHING ALMONDS AND CUTTING DRIED FRUIT

4 Tip almonds into a small bowl and cover with boiling water. Leave for 1½-2 minutes.

5 Drain almonds, put on to a plate and slide off skins between your fingers.

6 To cut large pieces of dried fruits easily, use kitchen scissors dipped in hot water.

4

TO PREPARE APPLE JACK

7 Dissolve icing sugar in hot water and spoon over cored apple. Sprinkle with cinnamon and bake in the oven set to 160C/325F/Gas 3 for 1 hour.

8 Put 2 heaped teaspoons of cooked apple pulp inside a glass and press against sides until smooth.

9 Add Calvados and apple juice to glass and then fill to within 2.5cm (1in) of rim with hot water.

7

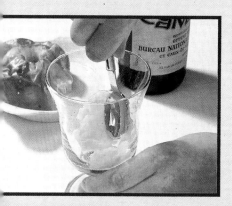

19

Apple Jack

Makes 1 drink

This apple drink is from North America and is laced with Calvados, France's apple brandy. Calvados is mainly produced in Normandy where it is used both in cooking and as a drink.

1 medium sweet eating apple
½ teapoon icing sugar
1 teaspoon hot water
Ground cinnamon
2 tablespoons Calvados
3 tablespoons apple juice
Sugar
Freshly grated nutmeg

EXTRAS
1 baking tray
Foil
1 heatproof glass or mug

1 Preheat oven to 160C/325F/Gas 3. Wash, dry and core apple then place on baking tray lined with foil.

2 Dissolve icing sugar in the water and spoon over apple. Sprinkle apple with cinnamon then bake in oven for 1 hour until soft.

3 Put 2 heaped teaspoons of cooked apple pulp into the glass or mug and press against sides until smooth.

4 Add Calvados and apple juice to glass then fill to within 2.5cm (1 in) of rim with hot water. Add sugar to taste.

5 Stir well to mix then sprinkle with nutmeg before serving.

DRINK YOURSELF WELL...
If you're suffering from the aftermath of flu, treat yourself to this vitamin-rich drink. Pour the juice of 4 freshly-squeezed oranges into a saucepan and heat until just hot. Mix in 2 tablespoons Amaretto (almond liqueur) and stir well to mix.

For a refreshing summer drink, don't heat the orange juice but serve chilled with the Amaretto and a few sliced strawberries in each glass.

Apple Jack

Playing with Fire

Makes 1 drink

A whisky and orange-flavoured treat.

3½ tablespoons whisky
3½ tablespoons boiling water
1 teaspoon icing sugar
Twist of orange peel

EXTRAS
2 mugs or 2 lemon tea glasses in stands
1 small saucepan

1 Preheat mugs or glasses (see step-by-step instructions on pages 18-19).

2 Pour whisky into small saucepan and warm gently but do not allow to boil.

3 Pour whisky into 1 mug or glass and water into the other.

4 Carefully set the whisky alight with a match. Pour into mug or glass of water. Pour back into the whisky glass. Quickly pour back and forth five or six times more and watch the flames dance between the mugs or glasses. Take great care and protect your hands with oven gloves. Decorate the glass with the orange twist and serve straight away.

SUCCESSFUL FLAMING
Warm alcohol flames more easily than cold but should never be allowed to boil. This is because the alcohol will be driven off and will not ignite. Hold flaming glasses with oven gloves for safety and don't stand too near.

Playing with Fire

Irish Coffee

Makes 1 drink

A delicately mild and finely-flavoured after-dinner classic.

3 tablespoons whisky
2 teaspoons brown sugar
1 cup of hot coffee
2 tablespoons whipped cream
Grated chocolate or chocolate curls to
  decorate

EXTRAS
1 heatproof stemmed glass
1 candle

1 Pour whisky into glass and warm with a
lighted candle, moving it round the
bowl of the glass.

2 Add sugar to glass then fill with coffee,
leaving 2.5cm (1in) clear at the top of
the glass. Stir gently to mix.

3 Gradually spoon over whipped cream
then decorate with chocolate.

USING CREAM
Cream for hot drinks should be the whipping
variety and beaten to soft peaks before
being spooned on top of the drink. If using
double cream, make sure the drink is sweetened or cream will immediately sink to the
bottom and turn the drink cloudy.

Irish Coffee

Scottish Egg Flip

Makes 1 drink

A well-known combination said to come from the Scottish Highlands.

2 tablespoons whisky
1 tablespoon Drambuie
2 teaspoons honey
1 egg, beaten
155ml (5fl oz/⅔ cup) milk
Freshly grated nutmeg

EXTRAS

1 cocktail shaker or vacuum flask
1 mesh sieve
1 heatproof glass
Saucepan
1 straw

1 Put whisky, Drambuie, honey and egg into a cocktail shaker or flask and shake steadily for 30 seconds.

2 Strain drink into glass through sieve.

3 Heat milk until hot. Gently stir into glass then sprinkle with nutmeg. Serve with a straw.

COLD NOG

Shake the first four ingredients with 4 ice cubes. Strain into a glass and top up with chilled milk.

EGG PUNCH

Put 3 cloves, 1 cinnamon stick and a 10cm (4ins) strip of lemon peel into a saucepan with 6 tablespoons water. Cover and warm over a low heat for 30 minutes, taking care not to let the mixture boil. Cool and chill. For each drink, separate 2 eggs. Beat yolks with 1 heaped tablespoon caster sugar until thick and pale cream in colour. Stir in 250ml (8fl oz/1 cup) chilled white wine then strain in the chilled spicy water. Whisk lightly, pour into a large tumbler and sprinkle top with freshly grated nutmeg.

Scottish Egg Flip

Indian Summer

Makes 1 drink

An autumn drink from North America.

Ground cinnamon
250ml (8fl oz/1 cup) apple juice or cider
2 tablespoons Calvados
1 cinnamon stick

EXTRAS
1 saucer
1 heatproof glass or mug
1 saucepan

1 Tip some ground cinnamon on to a saucer. Dampen rim of glass or mug and twist in cinnamon to give it a brown edge.

2 Pour apple juice or cider into saucepan and heat until hot but not boiling.

3 Carefully pour Calvados into glass, taking care to avoid the cinnamon-coated rim.

4 Gently fill glass with the hot apple juice or cider, stirring with the cinnamon stick.

AFTER A GOOD MEAL...
A digestive is often recommended. Try this: Pour 1½ tablespoons Amaretto into a glass and top up with coffee. Stir in sugar to taste.

Indian Summer

Night Cap

Makes 1 drink

Infinitely better than a hot water bottle or electric blanket.

250ml (8fl oz/1 cup) milk
4 tablespoons dark rum
1 teaspoon icing sugar
Freshly grated nutmeg

EXTRAS
1 saucepan
1 heatproof glass or mug

TO KEEP THE SPARKLE
Glasses filled with drinks containing milk, cream and/or eggs should be rinsed under cold water then washed with hot water and detergent before being dried. This will prevent cloudiness and a stale smell.

1 Heat milk in saucepan until just on the point of boiling then remove from heat.

2 Pour rum into glass or mug then add sugar. Stir in hot milk, sprinkle with nutmeg and drink straight away.

Night Cap

Tom and Jerry

Makes 1 drink

Rum and brandy form the basis of this heart-warming punch.

1 egg
1 heaped teaspoon icing sugar
250ml (8fl oz/1 cup) milk
2½ tablespoons dark rum
1 tablespoon brandy
Freshly grated nutmeg

EXTRAS

1 small bowl
Electric whisk
1 plate
1 small saucepan
1 small jug
1 large mug or heatproof glass

1 Separate egg. Beat white in a bowl until very stiff then pile on to a plate.

2 Put the yolk into same bowl and beat until very thick and creamy with the sugar. Gently stir in beaten whites to make a firm batter.

3 Heat milk until hot but not boiling.

4 Put batter into a pre-warmed jug and gently stir in rum, brandy and 3 tablespoons of hot milk.

5 Top up with remaining milk. Pour into mug or glass, sprinkle with nutmeg and serve straight away.

TIPS

1 A pinch of salt or dash of lemon juice added to the egg white will make it stiffen more readily.

2 Grand Marnier or Bourbon can be used instead of the rum.

3 For an exotic touch, sprinkle top with a pinch of garam masala instead of nutmeg.

Tom and Jerry